Our New Boat

BY ALYSSA KREKELBERG

We wait for
our new boat.

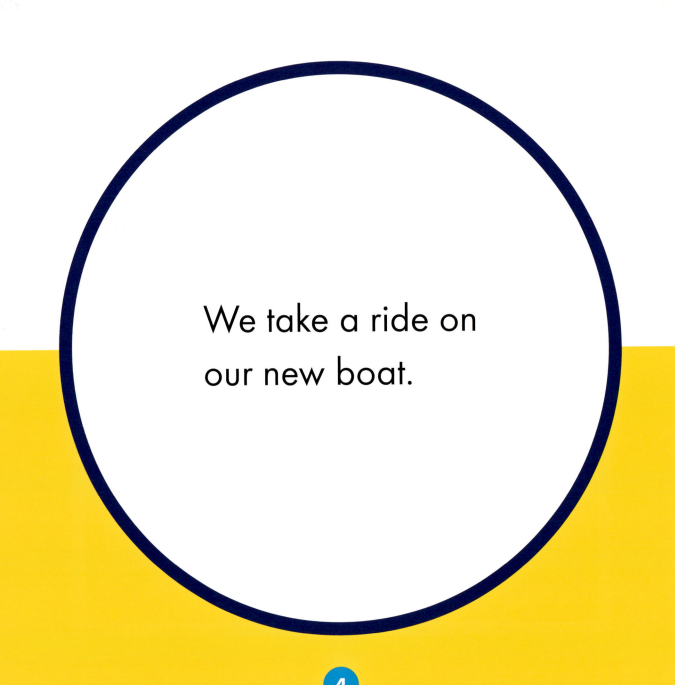

We take a ride on our new boat.

We go fast on
our new boat.

I stand by Dad on
our new boat.

Dad drives
our new boat.

We sit on
our new boat.

We see blue water
from our new boat.

Fish swim by
our new boat.

Ducks swim by
our new boat.

We are happy on
our new boat.

Note to Caregivers and Educators

Sight words are a foundation for reading. It's important for young readers to have sight words memorized at a glance without breaking them down into individual letter sounds. Sight words are often phonetically irregular and can't be sounded out, so readers need to memorize them. Knowing sight words allows readers to focus on more difficult words in the text. The intent of this book is to repeat specific sight words as many times as possible throughout the story. Through repetition of the words, emerging readers will recognize, and ideally memorize, each sight word. Memorizing sight words can help improve readers' literacy skills.

boat

new

our

23

About the Author

Alyssa Krekelberg is a children's book editor and author. She lives in Minnesota and enjoys exploring the great outdoors with her hyper husky.

Published by The Child's World®
1980 Lookout Drive • Mankato, MN 56003-1705
800-599-READ • www.childsworld.com

Photographs ©: iStockphoto, cover, 1, 2, 5, 6, 9, 10, 13, 14, 18, 21; Photo Home Page/iStockphoto, 17; Andy Works/iStockphoto, 23

ISBN 9781503835672
LCCN 2019943124

Printed in the United States of America